Usborne Beginners
Tadpoles
and frogs

Anna Milbourne

Designed by Nicola Butler

Illustrated by Patrizia Donaera

Frog consultant: Chris M...

Reading consultant: Alisa...

Contents

Frog eggs

In a quiet pond, a mother frog lays lots of little eggs in the water.

The eggs are called frogspawn.

Each egg is a tiny, black blob. Each blob can turn into a frog.

Baby tadpoles

Inside a frog's egg something is growing.

and bigger.

It starts as
a tiny dot.

It gets bigger

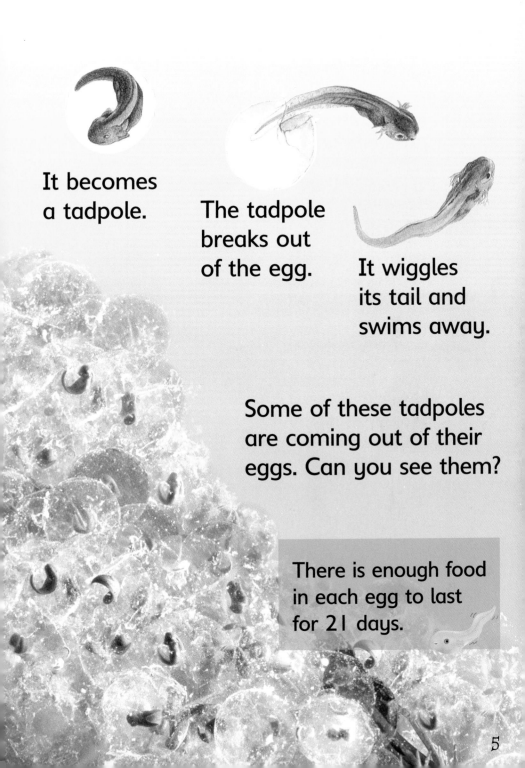

It becomes
a tadpole.

The tadpole
breaks out
of the egg.

It wiggles
its tail and
swims away.

Some of these tadpoles
are coming out of their
eggs. Can you see them?

There is enough food
in each egg to last
for 21 days.

5

Tadpole life

Tadpoles live in ponds and streams.

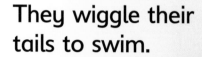

They wiggle their
tails to swim.

Tadpoles have tiny teeth
and eat pond weeds.

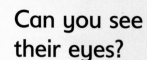

Can you see
their eyes?

Tadpoles breathe under the water using gills.

Gill—

Flap—

At first, the gills
look frilly, like this.

Later, flaps grow
over the gills.

Hungry fish like to eat tadpoles.
The tadpoles swim fast to get away.

These tadpoles are brown like the
stones in the pond. They can hide
so the hungry fish can't see them.

Growing up

As a tadpole grows up, it turns into a frog.
Follow the numbers to see how.

1. Two legs grow near its tail.

2. Next, two legs grow near the front.

One kind of tadpole grows up on its mother's back. It hops off after it has become a frog.

3. Its tail
gets shorter.

4. Soon its tail
has almost gone.

5. Now it has
become a frog.

Head to toe

Frogs have big eyes on top of their head. They can see all around them.

This is the frog's ear.

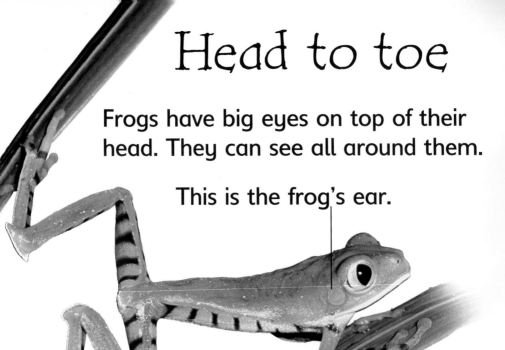

Can you see the frog's nostrils?

Different kinds of frogs have different eyes.

Some have heart shapes, slits or ovals in the middle of their eyes.

This is a
webbed
foot.

Many frogs have webbed feet. This means
they have skin between their toes. Webbed
feet help frogs swim fast.

Frogs aren't always green. They can be yellow
or blue or red. Some have spots or stripes, too.

Jump and splash

Frogs live on land and in water.
They have long, strong back legs.

Frogs don't walk to
get around. They jump.

A frog can jump twenty
times the length of its
own body.

How far can you jump?

This frog is diving
into the water.

Frogs are good
swimmers, too.

13

Dinnertime

Hungry frogs like to eat bugs and flies.
Follow the numbers to see a frog catch a fly.

1. The frog rolls out its sticky tongue.

2. The fly sticks to the frog's tongue.

3. The frog rolls its tongue back in.

4. The frog shuts its mouth with a snap.

Frogs swallow their food whole.
A frog's eyeballs bob down when it swallows.
This helps push the food down its throat.

Some frogs don't have long tongues.
They have to jump to catch their dinner.

This frog is jumping to catch
the bug before it crawls away.

Slimy and warty

Most frogs have wet, slimy skin. They don't drink water. Water goes in through their skin.

Frogs change their skin to keep it fresh. This is called shedding their skin.

The frog wriggles. Its old skin comes loose.

It pulls the skin over its head like a sweater.

It eats the old skin. The skin beneath it is new.

A toad is a kind of frog. Toads are different from other frogs. They have dry, warty skin.

A toad

Toads don't mind living in dry places. Some even live in the desert.

Hide-and-seek

Some animals like to eat frogs. Some frogs hide so they can't be seen and eaten up.

Can you see the green frog?

This green tree frog is hard to see on a leaf.

On a brown branch it is easy to see.

Its skin turns brown. Now it is hard to see.

These frogs are poisonous.
They don't need to hide. Their bright skin tells animals they are bad to eat.

 A single drop of poison from an arrow-poison frog's skin could kill you!

Frog tricks

Frogs have tricks to stop animals from eating them. If an animal bites a tomato frog, it gets a sticky surprise!

The snake bites the tomato frog. Sticky goo comes out of the frog's skin.

The snake's mouth fills with goo which tastes bad. The snake lets go. The frog hops away.

Many animals eat their dinner alive. The river frog pretends it is dead, so animals leave it alone.

These frogs
have marks that
look like big eyes
on their bottoms.

If they are in
danger, they show
their bottoms.

The frogs hope the fake eyes make them
look bigger and scarier than they really are.

21

Hot and cold

Frogs don't like cold weather. In the winter, lots of frogs go to sleep for a long time. This is called hibernating.

A frog finds a safe place to sleep.

It goes to sleep.
It sleeps all winter.

In spring it gets warm.
The frog wakes up.

Frogs don't like to be too hot or dry.

This frog lives in the hot, dry desert. It digs a hole in the sand. It stays there because it is cooler. It only comes out when it rains.

Some frogs freeze like ice cubes in the cold winter. In spring, they thaw out and wake up.

Frog song

When frogs grow up they come back
to the pond where they were born.

The male frogs sing
a croaky song.

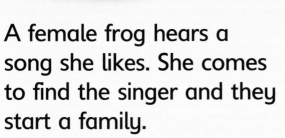

A female frog hears a song she likes. She comes to find the singer and they start a family.

This is how a frog croaks.

It puffs its throat up like a balloon. This makes a croaky noise.

The frog squeezes the air into its body. This makes another croak.

Frog homes

Frogs live in different kinds of places.

Many frogs live near
ponds and lakes.

This frog lives in someone else's home.

 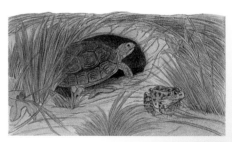

In the day, the
gopher frog sleeps in
a tortoise's burrow.

At night, the tortoise
comes home. Then
the frog goes out.

Some frogs live in trees.

They have sticky suckers
on their toes. These help
the frog stick to leaves.

—Sucker

Some frogs live in trees
their whole lives without
ever coming down.

Do you know if any frogs live near you?

Fantastic frogs

There are some
fantastic frogs in the world.

 This is one of the smallest frogs.
The picture shows its real size.

This is the biggest frog in the world.
It is called a Goliath frog.

It is about
the same size
as a pet cat.

This frog doesn't hop, it flies.
It uses its feet as wings.

It glides from
tree to tree.

This frog lays eggs and then swallows them.

The babies grow in
the mother's tummy.

Then they hop out
of her mouth!

Glossary of frog words

Here are some of the words in this book you might not know. This page tells you what they mean.

 frogspawn - the eggs a mother frog lays. They turn into tadpoles.

 tadpole - a baby frog. A tadpole grows up and changes into a frog.

 gill - a part on the side of a tadpole's head that it uses to breathe.

 webbed feet - feet which have skin stretched between the toes.

 warty skin - skin with lumps and bumps on it. Toads have warty skin.

 sucker - a pad which sticks to flat surfaces. Some frogs' toes have suckers.

 glide - to float along in the air. Some frogs can glide from tree to tree.

Web sites to visit

If you have a computer, you can find out more about frogs on the Internet. On the Usborne Quicklinks Web site there are links to four fun Web sites.

Web site 1 - Shine a light around to find all kinds of frogs in a forest and listen to them croak.

Web site 2 - Play a frog game.

Web site 3 - Print out pictures of frogs to shade in.

Web site 4 - Follow the pictures to make a jumping frog from paper.

To visit these Web sites, go to **www.usborne-quicklinks.com** and type the keywords "beginners frogs". Then, click on the link for the Web site you want to visit. Before you use the Internet, look at the safety guidelines inside the back cover of this book and ask an adult to read them with you.

Index

Acknowledgements

Managing editor: Fiona Watt, Managing designer: Mary Cartwright
Photographic manipulation by John Russell

Photo credits

The publishers are grateful to the following for permission to reproduce material:
© **Bruce Coleman** (Jane Burton) 26, © **Corbis** (Michael & Patricia Fogden) 10 (top),
(Joe McDonald) 17 (bottom), © **Corbis/FLPA** (Martin B Withers) 4-5, © **Corbis/Papilio**
(Mike Buxton) 11, © **Digital Vision** 10 (bottom), 31, © **FLPA – Images of Nature** (Minden
Pictures) 23, © **Getty Images/TCL** (Gail Shumway) Cover, 19, 27, © **J M Lammertink** 28 (top),
© **NHPA** (Daniel Heuclin) 28 (bottom), (Stephen Dalton) 28-29, © **Oxford Scientific Films**
(Alistair Shay) 2-3, (G I Bernard) 18, (Zig Leszczynski) 21, © **Tony Stone** (Tim Flach)
Title page, 13, (Christoph Burki) 16-17, © **Warren Photographic** (Kim Taylor) 6, 9, 14-15